Children:

The Ultimate Creation

After 30 years in downtown Boston, the new home of Hippocrates Health Institute is on a beautiful tropical estate in West Palm Beach, Florida.

Children:

The Ultimate Creation

●●●●●●

Anna Maria Clement & Brian R. Clement

with Foreword by Julia & Kenny Loggins

A.M. Press　　　West Palm Beach, Florida

©1994 by Brian R. Clement

Printed in the United States of America

Library of Congress Cataloging-In-Publication Data
pending

Clement, Brian R.
  Children: The Ultimate Creation
  ISBN 0-9622373-2-9

Cover and art illustrations by CAMF Productions
Typography and book design by Dianne Krause

Contents

Foreword

I met Brian and Anna Maria years ago, when I was 27, at the Hippocrates Institute. What drew me there was the first taste of success in a lifetime of struggling with a severe health issue.

My story is extraordinary because I was so sick for so long... and now I am strong and energized, able to dance with and sing to a child I never thought I'd have. My story is also simple, as simple as understanding what caused my physical body to break down in the first place.

I was born with what the doctors call an "undeveloped nervous system." This means my nerves were fried before I was born, from what had been an emotionally stressful pregnancy. My immune system was, therefore, also compromised.

By age 2, I had severe asthma and allergies. By 5, also arthritis in my hands, feet and hips. By 10, ulcers and hypoglycemia. By 15, migraines and the ulcers were bleeding. The asthma required daily adrenaline injections. I was allergic to all but eight foods, and every pollen, plant and flower. The doctors had prescribed dozens of experimental drugs, and I lost my hair twice.

In my early 20s, I was fortunate to be introduced by my first husband to the Fisher Hoffman Process — a program of individually guided emotional discovery, focusing on the first six years of life. I learned to identify the family patterns that created and perpetuated my illness. This work included the release of rage, grief and years of repressed feelings. I had been taught that I was sick, weak and crazy, and most damaging of all, powerless to heal. Over a year of intense work, I began to change this point of view.

My health improved, but I knew very little about diet and how it can also create and aggravate illness. I was also unaware of how food can regenerate the body to a state of vital and consistent health.

When I met Brian and Anna Maria , I was still overwhelmed by my health issues. But I had already experienced some big wins. We had discovered the Hippocrates diet through books and we had been using living foods, sprouts and wheat grass for six months, exclusively. My hypoglycemia was under control, and the ulcers were no longer painful.There my digestive system healed with the help of several juice fasts.

There was a strong desire to attend the Institute, since my physical healing had begun through their books. I spent several months at the Institute, taking the Health Educators Course and applying what I learned to my own healing process. My allergies diminished; my energy grew. So did my mental clarity and acuity. My physical strength was mirrored by a completely transformed sense of stability and well-being.

Mine is only one of the miraculous stories from the Hippocrates Health Institute. During my time there, I saw people arrive on stretchers with terminal prognosis from their doctors, and applauded as those same souls walked briskly out the door, sometime later — no canes, no wheelchairs — to new lives in new-made bodies.

I returned to Santa Barbara to open a healing practice, offering what I had learned to others. I was, of course, still healing myself. Within only two years, I went from being "allergic to life" to hiking miles in the hills, studying Tae Kwon Do, working 12 hours a day. What previously unimaginable feats! As I got healthier, I also felt more deeply what wasn't working in my marriage. We were friends and partners, but I was lonely and depressed. Our relationship lacked what Brian writes about here, something so important for children to experience in their parents. True love. We separated, and in the spring of 1990, Kenny and I fell in love. We were showered with a grace, a kind of love I had never seen or experienced. He had been my client, so I had already shared with him my understanding of physical and emotional health. His lifestyle put it to the test! Constant travel, stress, environmental toxins. "Earth Mother" meets the world! Without my wheat grass and sprouts, I couldn't have continued to heal and grow in so many ways.

Kenny discovered the emotional repercussions of sugar, alcohol and meat. His tender open heart would close and implode. Before our wedding he did a wheat grass and watermelon fast that he considers one of the "highest" experiences of his life.

What I wanted more than anything for a long time was to have a child. After three miscarriages, Anna Maria sent me a natural hormone therapy. I also dove into another type of emotional self-discovery led by a holistic teacher, Niravi Payne. I became pregnant, and found a talented chiropractor, acupuncturist and midwife to work with. Lukas Alushka Loggins was born at home, into his father's hands, on May 22, 1993. His drug-free birth was my spiritual rite of passage. Kenny and I were bonded forever and a family was born. I had a long labor, and afterwards my midwife said she marveled at my endurance and strength. Again, what an unimaginable feat!

Luke is our gift, our teacher and our reward. It is worth it. He's worth every ounce of wheat grass I ever drank! So are my three beautiful stepchildren, Crosby, Cody and Isabella. They teach us humility, respect, spontaneity and trust, and play, play, play! For them we are "growing out of" righteousness, rigidity, fear and control. Needing to know.

They are the new world. They deserve the best we've got to give. Brian and Anna Maria have been my teachers and friends for many years, and many of "the best" tools Kenny and I have come from their example. They "walk their talk," they are living proof of love and its fruit.

This book is from their personal experience of loving each other and raising children. They know what it's about, and write about the best of all possible worlds.

We trust you will take from this what feels right to you. Be gentle. Be compassionate. If the house isn't burning down, you don't need to focus all your energy on a fire. Integrate just what you can into your days. Parenting gives us many chances to do better next time. Love is the key.

Love,

Julia & Kenny Loggins
Mother & Dad
Songwriter & Musical Artist

Introduction

For most of our lives, we were ambitiously involved in creating a world of service for others. In the health field, we often find ourselves working long hours, going far past the maximum and often burning the candle on both ends.

The thought of a child for Anna Maria and me was far from our minds. Little did we know that children would become the center of our lives. Little did we know our education had not begun before we conceived our first little one. The experience of having a child has raised our awareness to different levels. We finally understand the true meaning of life and the importance of true love and harmony in a relationship.

We also understand the vital importance of rearing children in such a way that they are friends whom we can share information with and grow together. Anna and I are lucky friends and rewarded parents of three great children — a boy and two girls.

We often spend our moments of relaxation with our children, finding it to be the most rewarding and fulfilling time in our lives. We hope through the words that are written on the pages that follow, many people will feel what we now feel, and find a way in rearing children that is different from what our parents passed to us. In these generations, it is vitally important for all of us to become larger, to become more, and to share love.

Anna Maria and Brian Clement

Chapter One

●●●●●●

The Beginning: Love Equals Conception

Can we mold and build another human being? Can we instill the values that we hold dear into the heart of another? Can we teach a little body how to tie their shoelaces, read a book, understand the meaning of creation and be a constructive, productive, whole adult?

Obviously, we think we can. So we do. Guided by feelings of love for another, people want to create the actuality of that love. They actually want to show how deep that love is by creating another human being: to look in the face of that love, to hold them, feed them nurture them, teach them and watch them grow. Children embody all that love is: innocence, pure in motive and spirit, on Earth simply to give of themselves.

Conception itself is a spiritual process. It is the giving of two persons, transforming into an individual. It is the essence of the creation of all mankind, happening in small miracles all around the globe. It is not specialized to race. All races can recreate themselves. It is not specialized to religion, creed or philosophies of thought. Conception and creation are universal.

Chapter Two

●●●●●●

Am I Ready to Have A Child?
How to Know

F ar beyond the egg and the sperm, the DNA and the nine months of pregnancy, the mentality that prepares one for family must take place. Many feelings and emotions must be in order. Women and men have to reach within their souls and answer questions about themselves before having a child.

"Am I ready for a responsibility that lasts a lifetime? Can I effectively let my children become their own persons while guiding them along correct paths? Can I teach self-esteem? Do I know how to love? Do I love myself? Am I having this child for the right reasons?"

Not enough people ask themselves these probing inquiries, and even fewer answer honestly. A person must be in touch with his or her mission in life before creating another. They must be happy, content and whole, working to only make their lives more full before adding responsibility. For children are an immense responsibility. They are more than the money and the time and the effort.

It is the challenge of a lifetime: a daunting, imposing one for adults who are not ready; who are doing it for the wrong reasons; who did not have good role models; who are not spiritually and mentally in tune with the rhythms of the universe.

In almost all spiritual references, the purpose of humans is to re-create and multiply. It is an instinct that is buried deep within our souls. We must repopulate the earth, teach each other and love each other. But first, above all, we must love ourselves. Only then are we comfortable in the role we are about to embark on as parents. Sometimes this can be difficult, almost impossible. Oftentimes, people do not realize that they are lacking in self-love and self-esteem. Sometimes they are not taught clarity of purpose and decisiveness in mission or they've never been given the proper guidance and love in order to pass it on.

At the Hippocrates Institute, we can teach adult children the parenting which was never received.

Self-respect, self-care and self-awareness are all lessons that can be taught and learned at any age.

Many people think they will figure these things out later or the child will be their guide, as they grow with it. The child becomes their mission in life. That is wrong.

A mission is not a career or a job. It is not a role or an assignment. A mission is the reason we breathe, the wholeness and instructions we receive from a higher power. We are here to learn, to instruct, to love and grow, each in our own individual ways. Once people have carved out their role in the world, that is when they are able to pass on to a child what they have learned. When they feel good about why they are here and what they are doing, that is when they should start a family. When love is the basis of all their actions and health of both mind, body and spirit is their goal, that is when a child should be born.

It is then when conception will be easiest and peace of mind will be the greatest. But in this troubling time of violence, confusion and sometimes mass hysteria, the simple lessons of life — peace, understanding and respect — are lost. Children are born out of passion and desperation.

Chapter Three

●●●●●●

Teenage Pregnancies:
Lacking Children Born of Desire

T eenage pregnancies and children born from the stress inflicted by family members and that biological process abound. Instead of love and spirituality being the cornerstone of creation, women and men are relying upon physical desire and pressure to become families.

Teenagers are but children themselves, nowhere near the mental and spiritual whole that they are destined to be. Yet, in the U.S. alone, every year more than one million babies are born to teenage women not older than 18. A majority of these pregnancies are unplanned and undesired, conceived through the pressuring of an ardent boyfriend or the ignorant urgings of girlfriends who have already "done it." Nothing or very little in the way of love or respect has been taught to them.

Their thinking is muddled with adult passions and teenage peer pressure. They are insecure and lacking, feeding off whatever feelings are thrown to them through school, friends and the media. With this as a beginning, their children are insecure and lacking, too.

Although a small amount have miscarriages, the rest who become parents before their time suffer a wealth of problems. (1)

Emotionally, teenagers are ill-equipped to deal with the responsibility of being pregnant, much less becoming a mother or father. About one-third opt for abortion, the termination of a baby before it is born. The medical procedure of removing the fetus from the womb before viable is usually performed in the first trimester, when the risk of endangering the mother's life is low.

But an abortion is more than just a procedure. It is an act with deep emotional and spiritual relevance. Most young women who go through with the surgery do not realize the far-reaching, ever-present consequences of their actions.

About half of all the adolescents who have abortions are 18 or 19 years old. The other half are between 15 and 17; and a small number are 14 and younger. (2) But still hundreds of thousands of teenagers decide to give birth each year. They must then decide to give the baby up for adoption or keep the child and become parents. The enormity of these decisions for an adult can be overwhelming. So imagine the pressure a teenager must endure making the same choices, most likely with the added responsibilities of school, extracurricular activities and a possible job.

Imagine the lack of security, love or warmth while making this decision. Nothing is there to draw on: no source of support; no higher power providing help. Teenagers caught in this dire situation lack all resources. They are alone in every way imaginable — physically, psychologically, but most importantly, spiritually. They do not know the wonder of creation. No one has ever taught them. They do not know their mission in life. They haven't had the time to discover it. They do not know why they're having these babies.

Some say because they are lonely and want someone to love. With this attitude, their children suffer. Their guider and caretaker is taking from them, using them to fulfill a wish. Some say because they don't want to have an abortion. Still the baby suffers, brought into the world without a foundation of love. Some say because they are ready to become parents. But how can a teenager satisfy the spiritual and emotional demands of a needy child, when he or she is incomplete themselves? The foundation is absent and the reasoning is illogical. With this start, only failure can be realized, and yet another soul without support is brought into the world.

And still there are the health risks. A teenage mother is more likely to give birth to a premature or low birth weight baby. (4) Since a teen is still growing herself, it stands to reason that during pregnancy, her body will require extra care and nutrition. Teenagers also are subject to feelings of denial, extreme fear, depression, apathy or feelings of "nothingness" and loneliness. (5)

Teenagers should stop listening to outside influences during this turbulent time in their lives and begin a cycle of self-nurturing, hope and well-being. As hard as it may be, peer pressure should be ignored and that inner voice calling out for health and love should be given credence.

At any time in a person's life, one can make a change and discover why they were really meant to be on earth. A teenager is no less worthy of beginning that journey than an adult. And once a better understanding of mission and purpose and health and spirit are comprehended, the only path left is the right one: a path that will lead to children and family when it is time, when love and not desire creates a child.

Chapter Four

●●●●●●

"Ticking Clocks":
The Biological Pressure Cooker

On the opposite end of the spectrum are adult women who, rather than having an unplanned pregnancy, are being forced to conceive. Some are constantly encouraged by their families, filled with eager members more ready for babies than they are. Or inside their minds, mature women are hearing "ticking" biological clocks, reminding them that they will be of childbearing age for only so long. As with teenage pregnancies, conceived by desire and ignorance, children borne by older women, conceived by outer and inner demands, are born lacking. Their mission and that of their mothers are not clear.

"Why did I have this child?" ask women over the age of 35. Because it was socially demanded; because I was running out of time; to make my family happy; to have an heir; to leave my legacy to the world. All wrong answers. The right answer — to create living, breathing love. Because my life is full, under control and healthful. Because I wanted to share all of the world's secrets with another. Because I wanted to give. It is within our nature as humans to want children. To feel that need to carry and give birth is not foreign or wrong, but the world we live in must be correct. Or as correct as we can make it.

Children brought into a world who are not complete will suffer the stresses of their parents and the insecurity therein. They grow looking for what they were born without — stability, reassurance, acceptance and love. It is not a difficult puzzle to piece together. Without a strong base, the building or child may fall.

Also, as with teenagers, women over the age of 35 have added risks during pregnancy. Some experience decreased fertility. The odds of having a child with Down's Syndrome increase, along with the risk of high blood pressure, diabetes and cardiovascular disease. (6) These conditions can be a result of not only aging, but also of unhealthy lifestyles filled with toxic indulgences, artificial additives and negative thoughts.

Children born of the wrong incentives — passion and pressure — and their mothers statistically suffer more problems and complications. Unhappiness and confusion cloud judgments and spirits. Naysayers, pressures and those of ill advice should be shut out of the conscience and the dictates of nature should be obeyed. The Hippocrates Institute teaches this power to embrace nature and the rhythms of the earth. Communing with green energy and the sanctity of peace can help one realize their purpose and the purpose of creation. In today's society of winning, fighting, taking and dominating, just the simple freedom of thinking and realizing can be hard to do.

But when the time is taken, this lesson will be learned: The basis of conception should be love. A spiritual connection. A goal of happiness. A need to create a miracle. A child should be welcomed into warmth and love.

Chapter Five

•••••

Planning:
The Ultimate Expression of Love

W hen the circumstances are right and the spirit is calm and whole, planning begins. Planning for a child can take place months, even years, before conception. It is a time when mother and father can talk about what they want and expect.

If she has not already begun to do so, the mother should implement a diet that has its roots in greenery. Live, green plants filled with oxygen and chlorophyll should be eaten, along with a total vegetarian diet to insure a healthful body ready to be inhabited by a baby.

Current understandings of human nutrition have antiquated the time-honored advice to "eat lots of meat and dairy products, so the baby gets enough protein and calcium." It is important to have an adequate intake of protein and calcium during pregnancy; however, meat and dairy products are certainly not the right sources of these nutrients. All the protein and calcium required for human health, including during pregnancy and childraising, are available in the delicious foods that grow from the earth. (6a)

The six essential components of any healthy diet, especially that of a healthful pregnant woman, are carbohydrates, fats, protein, vitamins, minerals and water. All can be obtained from the greenery that exists around us.

Carbohydrates and fats can be derived from grains, vegetables, nuts, algae, sprouts, and fruits, etc.; it's easy for the pregnant woman to get enough each day if she enjoys her shalaos — and for the weight-conscious, they are not fattening.

Protein, the building block for almost all human tissue, can be obtained from grains, legumes (beans), green vegetables, nuts and seeds. Contrary to the advice given by well-meaning, but ignorant doctors, meat and dairy products are not meant for human consumption. They are alien to our bodies. Greenery is not.

Green vegetables, such as sprouts, are an excellent source of not only protein, but also of oxygen which is crucial to the healthy development of any body. At Hipprocrates, the body is cleansed and energized with a "green drink," consisting of the juices of sunflower and buckwheat sprouts, cucumber, celery, garlic and ginger. This is part of the diet that should be implemented even before conception takes place and continued with the guidance of a lopicious counselor throughout pregnancy.

Completing the six essentials, vitamins can be found in a variety of forms. Water-soluble vitamins are again in green, leafy vegetables, as well as citrus fruits and grains. Oil-soluble vitamins are abundant in yellow vegetables and melons. All-important minerals like potassium, sodium, iron, zinc, selenium, calcium and iodine are found not in One-A-Day, but in green, leafy vegetables, grains and beans.

The most dense source of minerals needed to carry out the electrical and chemical functions of the body are found in sea vegetables. Kombu, dulse and most importantly kelp and algae deliver the needed amounts and can easily be added to soups and salads.

Last, but not least, is water. Our bodies are 76 percent water. The baby floats in a sac of specially formulated water. It is very important for the pregnant woman to drink two to three quarts of distilled water daily. This may seem like an extraordinary amount, but taken in the form of pure water, fruit juices, "green drinks," watery fruits, vegetables, soups and salads, it will add up quickly. (6b)

Daily physical and mental exercise, such as walking and stress reduction, as well as stretching, should be practiced to maintain a balanced spirit and body. In utero, a child can pick up on the messages a mother takes in.

Before they are even born, a child can feast on a green diet and listen to the peaceful transcripts of spiritual thoughts and study. The Institute can assist a "pre-mother" in her diet and mental well-being while she is trying to conceive. Many children are lost to miscarriages or subjected to difficult pregnancies because the parents lacked the forethought to prepare their home of nine months beforehand.

The father's role can be one of support, joining the mother with her diet and exercise and being an emotional stalwart. He can also help add a daily dose of laughter and warmth that will help develop a child in good spirits and calm mind.

While some may shun the efforts of studying and preparing, feeling that birth should be a spontaneous gift from above, planning for a child is the ultimate expression of love, since every effort is being made to ensure a structured, readied environment for the new member. There is no confusion or shock, just anticipation and joy. In addition to spiritual and physical planning, taking care of the details of emotional synchronicity and even finances can ensure a family that will be ready for anything.

Questions such as "Will I be a good parent?" "Can I rear a happy child?" "Can I be a better parent than my mother and father?" will be asked to determine even if the couple should try to conceive. In a society where both partners work to make ends meet, couples may face financial obstacles unique in our modern times. (7)

Also, both members have to assure that they want a child at the same time. A younger woman married to an older man or a younger man to an older woman, for example, may not want to produce instant babies just so he or she can avoid being "a grandparent" to his or her children. Further, what two people agreed on before marriage, if they discussed children, may not be what they agree on after two to five years of married life. Even in good marriages, arguments occur over the number and timing of children. (8)

Planning also includes finding space in your home for a child, rearranging your schedule and relinquishing freedom and some activities. Money, career, goals, housing, insurance, transportation, and even relationships with friends, family and each other are called into question when anticipating a child. Everything changes. And no one can take all the changes into account.

But making the effort to learn all that you can about having a child — from what to eat while you're pregnant to how much college tuition may be — can lower the stress and dissolve some of the anxiety. The result will be a more confident couple, armed with knowledge, wisdom, peace, sanctity and control, ready to have a baby and concentrating on how to make that child and their newly expanded family as happy and as whole as possible.

Chapter Six

●●●●●●

Giving Birth the Natural Way

F rom the very beginning of their entrance into the world, children are living, breathing, hearing, feeling souls.

Their spirits and consciences are veritable blank pages, ready to be filled with lessons from loving, generous parents who are knowledgeable in the ways of the universe. As it has been stated before, no one is too young or too old to be on his or her mission. In fact, it is best for the plans to be laid as soon as possible to avoid the pitfalls of sickness, disillusionment and confusion. So the introduction into this world is a high priority.

Babies enter the world crying, shaking and cold: tired from a rough journey and separated from the warm, wet havens they called home for almost a year. The first thing they need is reassurance that security isn't far away. Babies should be told and shown right away that they are deeply loved.

From the moment labor begins, the whole family should be there: helping, coaching, encouraging. Even if the mother only wants to concentrate on one voice, for example her partner's or attendant's, the other family members should be nearby, letting their presence be a source of comfort.

The environment of birth should reflect the origin of birth. It is a natural process of giving, so all that is natural should be surrounding the mother. If the pregnancy is a well one, devoid of complications and risk, a setting filled with wholesome accessories is best.

A warm temperature, a homey setting (home or even outside), a water birth done in a tub of moving liquids, natural fibers, like cotton or linen, soothing, rhythmic music or environmental sounds, like crashing waves or a babbling brook. All of these things should be there to create a feeling of nature, like the woman is just joining in with the set patterns of the earth. The birthing process, though most often painful, should not be stressful as well.

To this end, a midwife (a woman trained to assist the mother to give birth) is the best option as an attendant. Male doctors, while well versed and thoroughly learned in the biological aspects of childbirth, have obviously never been through it. It is a spiritual, overwhelmingly touching process that they have never experienced. The contractions that slowly bring another being forth. The strain of pushing and breathing. The metamorphosis of the uterus and body. The euphoria as the child emerges and cries its first lusty sound announcing its arrival. None of this has a male doctor felt. Another woman has.

So she will be better able to read and respond to a mother's rhythms and more accurately understand what is needed and felt. A connection can be formed that will transcend the normal doctor-patient relationship and maybe last a lifetime.

After the strenuous task of birth, bonding should begin immediately.

Bonding, a new buzzword, signifies security and love. Bonding means the child and each member of the family creating a special relationship of trust and caring. In most cases, the first member to bond with the child after birth is their mother.

The baby should immediately be placed upon her stomach or chest so they can feel her warmth and hear the familiar heartbeat they grew with. Eye contact and the first attempt at breast feeding may also take place, letting the child know that they are among love and experiencing a very natural science.

From there, the father may hold his child, able for the first time to feel a creation that is half his. Looking into their father's face, smiling, laughing, or screaming, crying, the child will be "introduced" to an integral part of their life.

When children are born, all of their family should be in the room, taking part and giving support and love. It is within our humanity that carrying on the family lines bonds family members closer than anything else.

Even if the child is premature and separated from their family, bonding can still take place. It can happen later in the hospital bed, or through the portholes of an incubator, or at home. (9) If the mother is experiencing a medically complicated or risky pregnancy, a hospital is recommended for the child and mother's well-being. If an emergency occurs, such as a slowed or stopped heartbeat or breech birth, time is of the essence and medical assistance should be a hairsbreadth away.

If allowed, the mother and father should create as much as possible a natural environment within the hospital room. Music, lighting, blankets from home and familiar faces will suffice as long as the mental fortitude and calm spirit are present.

As long as the children know that they are loved, appreciated, welcomed, cherished and secure upon their arrival, the family will flourish.

Chapter Seven

●●●●●●

Eating Naturally for Mother and Child

I n previous chapters, it has been emphasized that the nutrition of the child begins before birth, even before the mother becomes pregnant.

A well-nourished mother, revitalized with the nutrients of "live foods" and exercising properly, translates into a well-developed child and a pregnancy that is normal and complete.

While the cliche ice cream and pickles-eating pregnant woman still exists, more and more women are studying their diets to achieve well-balanced menus of organically grown foods while they're nurturing their child within. The child will then take in the wholeness and energy found in the Hipprocrates diet.

Mothers-to-be realize early on that the vague instructions of "eat sensibly" may lead to lacking diets. And a lacking uterus creates a lacking child. Recent research on nutrition in pregnancy suggests that when diets are inadequate the result is that some babies die or are in poor condition, and some mothers have difficult pregnancies, labors and subsequent illness. (10)

If the mother half-starves herself or eats low-quality food, she deprives her baby, too. She is more likely to have a miscarriage and, if the pregnancy is maintained, the baby is more likely to be premature or of low birth weight. Inadequate nutrition in the later part of pregnancy can also affect the child's brain development. (11)

While most books and magazines on pregnancy offer a wide variety of dishes and menus, the mother should rely on her lifestyle, body and the rhythms of nature to shape her diet. What is required for the baby may differ from the first trimester to the third. Appetites ebb and flow, so does energy and even interest in food. Certain foods during the first few months of pregnancy may prove impossible due to nausea and morning sickness.

Instead, importance should be placed on consuming well-balanced meals with a majority of fruits, green vegetables and high-quality distilled water. Every pregnant woman is different. One may crave salty snacks. Another may crave pineapple. Each should concentrate on keeping her diet as organic and wholesome as possible.

Instead of chips, the pregnant woman should munch on soaked almonds, sunflower seeds, pumpkin seeds, sesame seeds or other nuts, except cashew or peanuts, which are high in sodium, aflotoxin and poison. Instead of just pineapple, vary the fruits with select organic, tree-ripened seasonal buys.

But remember to limit the intake of fruit to only 15 percent of the diet. When high or low blood sugar is at play, less or no fruit should be taken.

If the mother is receiving important prenatal care, her healthcare professional will probably prescribe a prenatal vitamin and possible iron supplements that supply the extra minerals needed for the child's development. In some cases, without these extra allowances, the child may take from the mother's system, depriving her of nutrition. Vitamin and mineral deprivation may lead to anemia, bleeding gums and fatigue.

NOTE: Pregnant women should investigate and ask numerous questions about the need to supplement their Hippocrates diet with a vitamin/mineral additive every day. A compromise should be encouraged if the necessary requirements are met with increased amounts of green vegetables and blue-green algae. A woman should inform her healthcare provider of her healthful living habits, "living" diet and mental maintenance before discussing any additions to her lifestyle.

Overly stringent rules for menu selections, however, lead to dieting stress and eventual rebellion. So, the mother should allow herself a compromise or substitution every now and then, but should always keep in mind the prize of her wholesome menu — a healthy, happy baby.

Once children are born, their nutrition should remain a responsibility of the mother. It is widely encouraged by the Institute, health practitioners and everything that is natural that a mother breastfeed her baby for at least the first two years of life.

Human breast milk contains at least 100 ingredients that are not found in cow's milk and that cannot be exactly duplicated in commercial formulas. Breast milk is individualized for each infant; raw materials are selected from the mother's bloodstream as needed, altering the milk's composition from day to day, feeding to feeding, as the baby grows and changes. Variations from breast milk in homemade cow's milk formulas can lead to nutritional deficiencies.

Breast milk is not more digestible than cow's.

Breast milk is less likely to cause overweight in infants, and obesity later in life.

Virtually no baby is allergic to breast milk (though some can have allergic reactions to a certain food or foods in their mothers' diets, including milk).

Nursed babies are almost never constipated because of the easier digestibility of breast milk. They also rarely have diarrhea — since breast milk seems to encourage the growth of beneficial flora in the digestive tract.

Breast milk contains one-third the mineral salts of cow's milk. The extra sodium in cow's milk is difficult for a baby's kidneys to handle.

Breast milk contains less phosphorus. The higher phosphorus content of cow's milk is linked to a decreased calcium level in the formula-fed infant's blood.

Breastfed babies are less subject to illness in the first year of life. Protection is partially provided by the transfer of immune factors in breast milk and in the premilk substance, colostrum.

Nursing at the breast, because it requires more effort than sucking on a bottle, encourages optimum development of jaws, teeth and palate.

Breast milk is safe. There is no risk of contamination or spoilage.

Breastfeeding is convenient. It requires no advance planning or packing, no equipment; it is always available and at just the right temperature. When mother and baby aren't together, milk may be expressed in advance and stored in the freezer for bottle feedings as needed.

Breastfeeding is economical. There are no bottles, sterilizers or formula to buy; there are no half-emptied bottles or opened cans of formula to waste.

It's been suggested that breastfeeding decreases a woman's risk of developing breast cancer later in life.

Lactation suppresses ovulation and menstruation, at least to some degree, though it should not be relied on as a form of birth control.

Nursing can help burn off the fat accumulated during pregnancy. If a woman is careful to consume only enough calories to keep her milk supply and energy up and makes certain that all those calories come from nutritious foods, she can fill all of her infant's nutritional needs while recovering her own figure.

Breastfeeding enforces rest periods for the new mother — particularly important during the first six postpartum weeks.

But most importantly, breastfeeding brings mother and baby together — skin to skin, at least six to eight times a day. The emotional gratification, the intimacy, the sharing of love and pleasure, can be very fulfilling. The spiritual bond that is created during these times last far beyond childhood, supplying a stable base of love and security. These moments of nurturing and care go past the biological and nutritional into the spiritual. There is no closer binding experience than feeding a child from your own body. It is the way nature intended. And it is also a way to insure that the child continues to receive the benefits of an organic diet, which should be carried on by the mother to speed the healing and recovery of birth.

Unfortunately, in North America, only four percent of women breastfeed their child until they are two years old. That two-year period is a necessity for the child to develop correctly with all its cells and bone structure building in order.

But more than supplying a physical, spiritual and emotional need, being naturally fed by their mothers also fills a psychological need for babies.

Without that bond, many children are brought up lacking what they need, which affects their response to society as adults. The number of children who are not breastfed until they are 2 years old—about 96 percent—become needy, taking, selfish and sometimes greedy. They are constantly in search of the element that was not there in their youth.

Imagine being deprived of the love and warmth so incredibly needed during a time when you are small and helpless and weaker than you will be at any other time in your life. Imagine only being given half the spiritual food needed for sufficient growth. Imagine hugs and kisses taking the place of being close to your mother, while you experience the most important ritual for survival—nourishment. It happens all the time. In fact, it is the norm.

This is why we have a "lacking" society. One that is always falling short of happiness, peace and fulfillment. If children are denied that first integral relationship with their mother, they are receiving the message that they are never going to get what they deserve, what they need.

So on a primitive, instinctual level, the child, as an adult, will start to take things to fill that large hole they have in their life: taking of other people's time, energy and faith. For a large majority of our society, unfortunately, this is how the spirit of a human being is initially molded.

A problem that is so big has a solution that is so small. Breastfeed your child. Let him or her take what is deservedly theirs. It is the lesson of all that surrounds us, from the animals to the trees, that the young feed from their mother. Take part in the patterns set up millions of years before our being and protect your generations with the fullest gift you can give: yourself.

Chapter Eight

●●●●●●

The Other Side of Natural:
When Breastfeeding Isn't an Option

F or some women, however, breastfeeding is not a viable option. They have to rely on bottle feeding because their bodies are unable to supply food for their baby.

The reasons may be emotional or physical, due to mother's health or the baby's. (13) The common maternal factors making breastfeeding ill-advised include:

Serious, debilitating illness or extreme underweight; serious infection, such as tuberculosis; conditions that require medications that pass into the breast milk and might be harmful to the baby, such as antithyroid, anticancer or antihypertensive drugs; AIDS, which can be transmitted via body fluids, including milk; drug abuse and a deep-seated aversion to the idea of breastfeeding. (14)

The last reason is not a real reason, though. It is a mental by-product of society's conditioning that breastfeeding is unacceptable. That it is not sociable or comfortable. Many believe that a bottle, with its cold, lifeless shell, can adequately replace a living, loving human being. That is not true. At the Hippocrates Institute, lecturers and counselors can help those of this mentality overcome the barriers that prohibit them from accepting nature. It is not something to be embarrassed about. It is something to relish in.

Other factors that may restrict breastfeeding may be if the mother smokes more than 20 cigarettes a day. Nicotine is a drug which, delivered to the baby in milk, may cause restlessness, nausea and vomiting. Smoking that number of cigarettes a day may also reduce the amount of milk the mother produces. (15)

Smoking. Drug use. Society-induced sickness. All of the suffering is a matter of mentality, of asking yourself "Do I want to poison my body? Do I want to limit my physical capacities? Do I want to cloud my judgment with how to get another cigarette or fix?" The answer is no. Many trained professionals can help a person stick to that answer and help them change their lifestyles to live that answer.

Ridding the body of toxins and waste will enable it to work in improved condition, helping the soul it houses along the journey of life. On a smaller scale, a healthy body can supply food to a child, and the child will benefit greatly from their mother's choice for a better, cleaner life.

From the baby's side, disorders like lactose intolerance and phenylketonuria — in which neither human nor goat's milk can be digested — or a cleft lip may prohibit breastfeeding. (16)

About one-third of women suffer from these conditions that keep them from physically breastfeeding. But for the rest who do not, breastfeeding can be the sole source of nutrition until the baby is 24 months old. At that time, organic fruits pureed with high-quality distilled water or reverse osmosis water can be introduced.

Chapter Nine

••••••

Starting Solids:
The Next Step in Nutrition

I n a majority of cases, over-eager parents feed their children solids, such as rice and oatmeal cereal, too soon.

Some mothers insist on feeding their children solids just days after they are born — a poorly conceived tradition that dates back to the eighteenth century. (17) Unfortunately, the infant's digestive system is not prepared to handle the task of breaking down anything more complex than breast milk, which is custom-designed to be easily digestible.

The immature intestinal tract of the young infant is incapable of screening out the larger, more complex molecules that come with solid foods and that may lead to allergic reactions. As any parent knows, it's not normal for a baby's nose to run constantly or for a fever to keep reoccurring. It could be because solids or the wrong kind of solids were given too soon.

Availability of the food, getting the baby to sleep through the night, ensuring the child is growing properly and jazzing up the "drab" diet of milk are some of the most prevalent reasons mothers start solids too early. (19) Others respond to society's message that babies should be plump and chubby. Each reason can be disqualified with one simple reply: the child, not the parent, determines when they are ready for something more substantial.

When eight ounces of milk doesn't suffice for longer than three hours and the child wails in hunger, a heavier diet may be needed. As to adding cereal to a bottle: Adults would not eat cereal lying on their backs and neither should a baby. Wait until the baby has the muscle strength and coordination to be able to hold his head up, which means he or she should just about be able to sit on their own. (20)

Even vegetables should not be introduced before their time. In fact, the only variance from a milk diet should be juice, added around the 20th month. Organic raw apple juice, as an example, since it is derived from just one fruit and not a combination, is the best to start with.

The next item on the menu should be vegetables—not only to delay the child's inevitable love of sweets from fruits, but to also supply the inherent oxygen found in vegetables. The body will recognize its need for oxygen input and demand such green and yellow organics as green beans, squash, sweet potato, peas and avocados. Such foods supply protein, calcium and other essential nutrients, while preparing them for a vegan diet of green and sprouts later.

All of the elements of the baby's diet should mirror that of the adult's diet. It should be green, from the earth, organic and oxygen-filled. Nothing should interrupt the flow of continuity in the transference from breast milk to solids. Energy should be at the base of children's menus re-establishing the utero environment of live food they received from their mothers and natural world in which they live.

To disrupt the flow now, at a developmental stage, would hinder future physical and mental development, as well as weaken the base for the creation of a whole and satisfied adult.

Inherent to a developing child's diet are calcium and protein. Again, mother's milk provides both elements in their entirety, but upon leaving the breast, protein should come from sprouts and other naturally grown foods.

Fresh water algae, a source of protein, minerals, vitamin, and oxygen, can be introduced at 2 years old. Children need very little to meet their needs, which are about 1/4 teaspoon per day at 2 years old, adding 1/4 teaspoon each year afterward until age 5. At that age, one teaspoon is sufficient for a well-maintained lifestyle.

Fresh water blue-green algae (Super Blue Green, chlorella) also supply important trace minerals and electrolyte factors often missing in today's diets.

Guiding the child on the correct path of nutrition is crucial. Patterns are established early, whether they be of consuming wholesome, organic foods or consuming empty, salt- and sugar-filled calories. In teenage and adult years, any routine that was begun in infanthood will continue, and separating from that routine will be difficult at best.

So it is wise to foresee the child's diet when they are 10 years old while they are 2 months old, and picture them healthy and whole or sickly and lacking. At this time in their life, more than any other time, children rely heavily on their parents to make the correct decision regarding their health and mental and spiritual well-being. It is not a decision to be made carelessly and in vain.

Just picture an adult who is suffering from physical maladies, a stressed-out existence, no mission and no love. Then picture adults at peace with their role in the world, searching for a higher meaning of our place here, in tune with the rhythms of the universe, happy, whole and taking what they need to survive from the earth itself. These people are your children based on your choice.

The choice should not be hard to make.

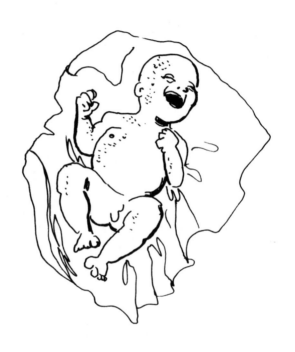

Chapter Ten

●●●●●●

**Footnotes to Food:
The Dangers of Overfeeding**

P ast what a child eats, a parent should make note of how much a child eats. Overfeeding is a recurring problem that leads to obesity, lethargy and subsequent unhappiness.

Most of us have the idea that more is better. More is stronger. More is bigger. But in reality, more food being fed to an infant translates into overkill and overload of their premature system. When babies are forced to eat more than they need, their bodies become exhausted simply ridding themselves of excess food.

As in beginning solids, parents should take cues from their children and only feed them when they are hungry. Children are not given enough credit from their caretakers for gauging their own appetites.

Mothers who overfeed their children do so because they are trying to meet needs other than hunger in their child through food. A baby's who's fed for all the wrong reasons (when she's hurt or unhappy, when her mother's too busy to play with her, when she's bored in the stroller) will continue to demand food for the wrong reasons. And as an adult, will eat for the same wrong reasons. (21)

Instead of nursing her each time she cries, comfort her with a hug or a soothing song. Instead of always plying her with teething biscuits, attach a toy to her stroller to keep her occupied. Despite what her grandmother's generation may have believed, constantly pushing food on a baby is not a sign of love. (22)

In some ways, pushing children to eat dooms them to a life as unhappy, overweight adults whose vibrations and cues are totally disturbed by the constant reminder of their failure as healthy human beings. Talk shows, reams of books and even more therapists have been employed to help "overweight" people find happiness and security within themselves. But does anyone stop to think how they got there?

It began long before the diets and the aerobic classes and the fad tricks. It began in the mind as a child, when mom or dad demonstrated that more was the way to go; that more food would make them happy and whole, when it was the opposite. It was more living that would do the trick, only mom and dad, who probably suffered from a low self-image themselves, did not know that. The cycles of such abuse and misinformation often bring people to the Hippocrates Institute for a way to "stop the madness," to ensure that they do not do this to their child.

Parenting instruction has to begin somewhere so that the cycle of good advice and healthful living can perpetuate itself through the generations.

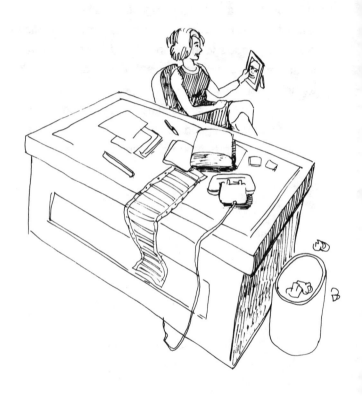

Chapter Eleven

●●●●●●

Juggling Mothering with Working

Responsibility.   That is the key to caring for a baby. A wealth of decisions await an adult who wishes to become a parent and as much as possible, they should be the right choices.

How will we pay for his food? Which doctor will she go to? What kind of food will she eat? What kind of toys should we buy? How soon should we start investing for his education? What kind of school should she attend?

But the root of responsibility is what kind of time will be spent with the children and who will shape their personalities and consciousness and teach them the lessons of life.

Traditionally, the weight of that question has fallen upon the mother — the parent who is the primary caretaker while the father leaves home to earn a living. But in today's society, both parents work. And while that role is customary for the man, the mother is left with divided feelings of wanting to fulfill her modern role as a professional career person, but also wanting to fill that traditional space as full-time mom.

The inner struggle also has to do with the instinctual role the mother wants to fulfill. She knows that her child looks to her for guidance and love and to be elsewhere other than with her child during this time of development goes against all that she feels and knows. It is difficult to fight the lessons of society, but it is even more difficult to fight the voice from within. The one that tells a mother not to leave the baby she carried for nine months and nurtured from her body. The one that tells a mother that her baby needs her. The one that tells her that no one will love and care for and know her child the way she does.

The decision to return to work can be met with excitement and optimism, as well as tears, frustration, anger and sometimes fear. What if my child is hurt and I am not there? What if the baby cries out for their mother and I'm at work? The emotions surrounding this decision are intense. As always, when confronted with a seemingly overwhelming problem — instinct versus intellect — the mother should listen to her soul and heart and rely on a higher power to show her the way.

If the money is needed and work provides fulfillment that is crucial to keep the mother happy, then returning to work should be a serious option. Or if the financial and emotional situation permits, part-time work, freelancing or a career change could meet both needs.

Working mothers have to be brilliant jugglers, keeping all the balls in the air at once. Yet even those who have found original ways to cope, wonder if the strenuous demands on their energy are costly to their children and careers and to their marriages. (23)

Says Judith Langer, a New York City market researcher who observed discussion groups of first-time moms, many of whom had or wanted careers: "They mentioned the word 'guilt' almost as often as the word 'baby'." (24)

The working women Langer talked with felt guilty about leaving their children and also guilty when they didn't miss them. Those who chose to stay home felt guilty about not working. Other anxieties included guilt about baby-sitters, about not giving enough to their partners, about their partners helping out too much, about taking time for self, about not working hard enough or working too hard on the job. (25)

If given a choice, most women would choose to stay at home with their children — at least for the first two years.

Yale University conducted a study with highly educated women at the top of their class from the U.S. and Canada and found that the majority answered that they would rather have a child than a career. The study concluded that it is an instinctual desire to have children, not the top management spot in a Fortune 500 company.

But whether a mother chooses to entrust her child to a caretaker, work part-time and try to meet both desires, or totally give up her career for a couple of years, her goal should remain the same: developing a healthy, whole human being. Such a goal is of benefit not only to the individual family, but also to the human race as a whole.

The spirit of the mother, the child and family hinge on this decision; therefore it should be a family decision with input from everyone. The bottom line is happiness begets happiness and unhappiness begets unhappiness, and stress and pain and clouded missions of life. Whatever creates the peace of a whole, working family striving for unity and love should be what is pursued. No one way of living a life is better than another if happiness is not at the core of the decision.

Look within and do what will bring harmony, satisfaction, love and security in the greatest degrees.

Chapter Twelve

●●●●●●

Raising Lesson No. 1:
Praise and Encourage

C ommunicating with children is an art. Unlike talking with adults, each session shapes the way they see themselves, how they will deal with others and their relationship with their parents.

Each situation is different. Praise differs from criticism. Instruction and encouragement differ from simple conversation. However, each interaction must share a common thread.

The child must know that the parent respects him as a person with his own feelings, opinions and experience. Toward this end, a child will grow up knowing that his voice means something and that he has the intelligence and character to take control of his life. He can know that he is of worth and important enough to want the best for himself in mind, in body and in spirit.

Parents have to remember that their audience is not as sophisticated as that of adults, but more sensitive and perceptive. So their words should be clear and beneficial, loving, instructive and spiritual. Sarcasm can leave a child confused and hurt, as can innuendo and inferences, which can lead to insecurity, mistrust and timidness.

For example, when a child's room is messy and the parent wants him to clean it up, saying, "I guess this person likes a dirty room," will not be as effective or as meaningful as saying, "Would you please pick up your toys and straighten your bed? I would appreciate your help in keeping our home neat and orderly."

Hurtful words, such as name-calling and insults, are extremely harmful and should be banned because their effect remains with a child long after the actual words are said. Children will repeat them to themselves until their self-esteem is diminished and their confidence is nonexistent.

Dooming themselves to fail, children set the scene for more criticism and vicious cycles of ridicule that lead to depression and stunted mental and emotional growth. How can children learn to embrace life and all the positive, healthful things the world holds when they do not have the love of self?

It was discussed in Chapter 2 that parents, before they even become parents, should examine their capacity of self-love and esteem. That process could be eliminated totally if a child is taught early in life that to love oneself is the key to happiness and peace and the art of loving others, including their own children. As babies, children pick up on cues to suggest their value. If parents treat children as priceless and expensive, then the children will see themselves in a positive light and want to learn how to preserve that light. It all begins with sincere, loving words of praise and encouragement.

A parent should also be aware of when criticism is constructive and destructive. Constructive criticism, which is an effective means of instruction and discipline, confines itself to pointing out how to do what has to be done, entirely omitting negative remarks about the personality of the child. When things go wrong, it is best to deal with the event, not the person. (26)

For example, when a child breaks a glass or makes a mess, it is best not to call the child clumsy or messy, but to help them set things right. Through actions, the child will learn to watch themselves more carefully and not blame themselves too harshly when things go wrong. Their parents don't dislike them because they broke a glass—they showed them so. So why should they dislike themselves?

Hurtful words, in any form, spoken to rectify a situation, in fact do the opposite. They perpetuate the opposite of spiritual work. Words to children should always be of happiness, love and honest education. What they hear is what they shall repeat and rely on.

If you tell them they are beautiful, they believe they are beautiful. If you tell them they are smart, they believe they are smart. And in believing this, they will do all they can to live up to their expectations of themselves. They will eat well because that is what smart, healthy people do. They will study the lessons of life because intelligent children want to know these things.

And they will love because they are being loved and cherished and admired and their world is good and whole.

Chapter Thirteen

●●●●●●

Raising Lesson No. 2:
Freedom for Healthy Development

Constructive communication is not always about what we say. The old adage "actions speak louder than words" still holds true, especially when trying to relay trust and confidence in your child. Therapist Glen Dolman found this to be true more than 40 years ago while studying the effects that "over-parenting" had on children.

Dolman worked with both mentally and physically challenged children and found that not all of them suffered from impairments. About half who had dysfunction suffered not from a physical condition, but from the training from their parents.

In an over-protection mode of parenting, the adults inhibited or stunted the children's growth, which led to mental problems.

Dolman's research included worldwide studies of child rearing and the relationships between parents and children. He looked at what the children did, what they ate, how they moved and retreated. He studied communities and tribes and found that parents must trust their children enough to let them explore.

Children must be allowed the freedom to wander and travel on their own. With this experience, confidence and growth — both mental and physical — will occur.

In studying two tribes, Dolman reported on one that would never let their children touch the ground. They were always holding the children and carrying them around. The other tribe would let the children run free and discover.

The difference in the children was that there was a massive amount of underdeveloped brain tissue or brain damage in the children that were constantly picked up and not allowed to crawl. With the other tribe's children, the levels of intelligence and confidence were much higher. Dolman attributed the disparity to the amount of freedom each tribe allowed and encouraged. He also ascertained that increasing the levels of independent exploration in healthy children would enhance their learning abilities even more.

In essence, not all mysteries of life can be taught by another, even if the teachers are mom and dad. For healthy development, some lessons must be — and should be — learned alone.

Parents have to set their children free in order for them to test the lessons they have learned. They have to experience the failings and triumphs of life to understand the relevance of their parents' instruction. How will a child know that greasy, fast food is bad for the body unless they venture out and see the effects for themselves? How will they learn about the dangers of drugs, smoking, overindulgence and inactivity if they do not see the detrimental effects it has on others?

How will they know that their life filled with wholesome, organic foods, daily exercise and mental dexterity and spirituality is superior to the life of unhealthfulness and spiritual ignorance led by a majority of society?

Children must also learn to trust their own judgment and rely on their instincts and schooling to get them through life. It is important that they learn independence so as not to be wrongly influenced by others later.

Let your children live life, not from the security and safe haven of your arms, but on their own sturdy legs and from their own vantage point. If the parenting job has been done well, they will not stray from the healthy, spiritual way of living taught them.

Chapter Fourteen

●●●●●●

Raising Lesson No. 3:
Self-Esteem and Self-Beauty

Who a child becomes is not determined in high school. It doesn't happen in college or while he earns a living and raises a family.

A majority of who children are is shaped during the first six years of their lives. In fact, 85 to 90 percent of his or her personality development takes place while they are enthralled with Dr. Seuss and running around on stretching limbs and smiling with a gap-tooth grin. It begins on the day of conception and starts to wane at about six years of age.

And it has to do with whether they receive love or not and whether they are allowed to live out their destiny: Independence.

With independence and confidence, children can venture out and experience the difficulties, trials and joys of life that will shape their opinions, influence their adult choices and color the way they react to society.

It is the parents' job to let their child go, and when the child returns, to reinforce the positive feelings of self-esteem and curiosity. Parents should encourage their child's strengths and assist them to improve their weaknesses.

By hearing "You are beautiful, you are successful, you are smart," an inner strength will grow and soon children will give that message to themselves. A positive self-image will lead a young person away from the dangers of drugs, crime and peer pressure because they are the by-products of lacking, weak self-image that teaches the child that they are bad, useless and worthless.

Discipline is also very important at this stage because children will test their independence and push for a level of autonomy separate from their parents. A parent should not be hurt by this new-found assertiveness, but find ways to work with it to benefit the child. Establish guiding strength, but do not stamp out their spirit.

This can be done in the following ways:

Instead of telling children what not to do, tell them what to do. Don't wait until they've made a mistake before you point out the correct way of doing things. This way, the instruction is perceived as instruction, not criticism.

Set an example. "Do as I say, not as I do" never works. If a parent wants his child to eat well, he or she should eat well and explain the advantages. If the parents want their child to read, they should read and explain the advantages. The same goes for exercise, relationships, responsibility and respect. Setting an example and supplying reasons for such behavior will make the child less susceptible to peer pressure. He or she will have an explanation, a platform and a goal for living. It is easier to develop with understanding than with an unsupported notion.

Allow the child to fail. The most difficult problem in being a parent is allowing your children to make the same mistake that you might have made. People seem to need to learn things from experience. It is called trial and error.

A child is human. And like their parents, will need to realize that if something does not work for them, then maybe that something was not meant for them.

All of this will teach children to lean on themselves, be responsible for their actions and be loving human beings. Self-esteem and self-beauty are two of the most important elements of a personality. Without them, a soul cannot venture outside of their own self-pity and insecurity to learn the wonders of life, the universe and their place in it.

People who care nothing of themselves will not take care of their bodies or feed their minds. A person that has no self-pride or self-worth will not seek answers, take risks or better their existence. A person without self-love will wither away in a morass of darkness, sadness and loneliness that leads to sickness, abuse and unhappiness. It is the basis of life to love. And everyone has to start with love of self before they can venture forward, become independent and truly breathe.

It is the parents' utmost responsibility to instill such love in their child. If they do not have the self-love to teach, they must embark on a journey to find it. We have practiced these simple truths with our children and students for decades.

Chapter Fifteen

••••••

The Teenage Years:
Mutual Respect and Communication

When children leave youth and enter adolescence, a myriad of changes take place in the relationship they have with their parents. New topics like sex, drugs, peer pressure, education and responsibility take over during family conversations, and efforts must be made to keep the lines of communication open.

Sex is usually a difficult subject for most parents. They feel clumsy, embarrassed, awkward and unsure about discussing such intimate acts with their children. How does a parent say "intercourse" and "kissing" to their teen without blushing, coughing or just leaving the room?

First, they have to overcome their fears and realize what they're about to say is important. And that conquering the fear of seeming inept may save them from the fear of dealing with an unwanted pregnancy, the threat of AIDS, an annihilated self-image or an emotionally torn child or grandchild.

Second, parents need to remind themselves that sex is a natural process. Without it, mankind would not exist. No one would be here. And that it is a process governed by a higher power that was meant for human beings to create life.

Many adults are resistant to discussing sex with their teens because they never had a comfortable, one-on-one talk about the subject with their own parents. Sex was discovered like a new land through misinformation from buddies in locker rooms or rumors from sisters and girlfriends at slumber parties. The wrong information was spread until someone experimented, found that it didn't work that way and was forced to be an example for others.

Teens today are more sophisticated and more are having sex earlier, with or without their parents' input. According to recent survey data, it is estimated more than half of unmarried girls have intercourse before they are 20, and that more than half of the unmarried teenage boys are sexually active by 19. (27)

They are exposed to sexual images from the time they turn on the television to the minute they pick up a magazine. And without the parents recognizing this fact, understanding the importance of arming their children with knowledge and overcoming their own anxieties, their adolescent — who is on the brink of adulthood and all its complexities — will never feel comfortable telling their parents their feelings.

He or she, like their parents, may grow up taking in inaccurate accounts of how sex and relationships should be. Parents should also know that long before their children become teenagers a form of sex education is already taking place.

Says V. Masters and N. Lehman in *Masters and Johnson Explained:*

Sex education should begin as soon as youngsters are old enough to observe their parents relating to each other. I don't think you have to "teach" them anything. If there is real warmth and interpersonal exchange in the marital relationship, the kids absorb it; some homes teach all the biology in the world, but the kids never see Mom and Dad holding hands. The point is that parents can and should demonstrate to children the importance of an effective and outgoing sexual relationship. (28)

In short, parents must present a loving, genuine relationship to their children for them to understand what a healthy relationship is truly about. Parents who show affection, share their thoughts and feelings, and demonstrate friendship and support for each other will be setting a promising example for their children.

A lion's share of the problem that children experience comes from watching the destructive relationship between their parents, with one parent belittling the other and dragging the child in between. In a truly giving partnership, teenagers can watch a love in action: how there is a sharing of the spirits, communication, sacrifice and attention; how the hard decisions are made with both voices; and how a disagreement is solved without destroying the other's self-esteem.

If the parents do not display this kind of love, the child's first relationship will most likely be an unhealthy one because in today's society control, rather than love, is stressed as the basis of interactions. And control-centered relationships lead to abuse, neglect and sometimes violence.

It is this silent kind of communication, setting an example, that will most influence teens looking for cues on how to live their lives.

When talking to teenagers about sex, parents should be conscious of listening as well as explaining. Listening is a key element in conversation. Without exercising that art, things are assumed, guessed at or misconstrued. If parents actively listen, the teen will guide them along the path to supportive direction.

At this stage, more than any other during their lifetime, children need to feel that they are in control, not their parents. They want to come to their parents for guidance and help in making their own decisions.

Unfortunately, "in knowing what's best" many adults try to resume the role they had when their child was young and take the reins. This power play leads to a disintegration of communicative lines. In establishing control and taking responsibilities for their actions, teens will naturally rebel against some of their parents' orders. This is normal. If a child agreed with everything the parent said, that would be abnormal because they could be holding their true feelings in for fear of reprisal, disappointment or confrontations.

Drawing the lines of control and freedom has a lot to do with understanding the teenager and recognizing when it is defiant disrespect and unruliness underlying their actions or just a testing of boundaries that have all of a sudden become too small. When trying to relate to a teenager it is best to try to walk a mile in their shoes. For adults who have forgotten life as a teen, here are some suggestions: (29)

Attempt to remember your own teenage experiences in order to better relate to and understand your teenager's problems.

Be considerate, realizing that the problems your teenagers are experiencing are as important to them as yours are to you.

Listen to their concerns and offer them the same attention you would give your adult friends.

Be patient while they try to tell you about their problems. Make no rash decisions or offer suggestions until you have heard them out.

Before you offer your suggestions, be sure that your teenagers are asking for advice. They may not want anything other than for you to listen for a few minutes. So take the time to listen before you react.

When the occasion is compatible, parents may also have the opportunity to present life, in general, in proper perspective with the teenage world. Teenagers should be made aware that learning to handle problems widely affords a strong basis for understanding and dealing with adulthood. The teen years are the proving ground for coping as an adult.

But if lines are broken, even after this introspection, parents should seek help and not blame themselves. About 60 percent of the population does not have healthy communication with their parents. Sometimes, part of the blame rests with the child.

Children who have supportive, caring parents can choose not to take advantage of that care. They can ignore it or abuse it, and, in turn, become self-destructive people. Other forms of abuse that children can inflict upon themselves include establishing unhealthy, intense sibling competitions and taking life cues from destructive peers.

When a child takes a turn in those directions, the parents can solicit advice from different sources and should not attribute the wrongness of their child's behavior to poor parenting.

But in the best of circumstances, respect and communication will solve most of a family's ills. All that was taught before birth, during infanthood and in youth — independence, exploration, spirituality, self-esteem, self-love — will begin to blossom during this time as teenagers aggressively seek to stake their claim in life, breaking away from parents and family members.

Staying in their corner while they grow and rebel and even surprise is the key to their stability, because even as young adults they need the support and stability that comes with being part of a loving family.

If they feel you respect them and listen to their desires and hopes, they will appreciate the efforts and try to return them. Explain that life itself is a two-way street of giving and taking, of relinquishing and receiving and that with understanding and hope, anyone can overcome diversity and miscommunication. They can even overcome the teenage years.

And at the end of the journey, when the family is a group of adults, all will have a meaningful relationship based on mature feelings of admiration and love.

Chapter Sixteen

●●●●●●

The Teenage Years:
The Importance of Bodies and Diet

C ell-body image, looking good, feeling good and being accepted are all extremely important as a teenager. Look at the teen magazines. On its pages, every boy is handsome, athletic and strong. Every girl is pretty, popular and slim. It is the teenage dream to have a body and face that conforms to society's picture of perfect.

Although the majority of children cannot achieve this feat, steps can be taken and should be encouraged to promote a healthy body and to help children accept the body they have been blessed with. Before the teen years, when a child is 11 or 12 years old, parents should find ways to incorporate regular exercise and well-body maintenance into their daily routine.

Parents should try to "practice what they preach" and ask their children to join them in daily walks, aerobics, stress-releasing exercises or a game of basketball. Dancing with their parents is a good way to exercise, too, because music can open their minds, souls and spirits and give them a format to express their true feelings. In exercising with their parents, children do not have to look far to find someone in good physical condition to emulate.

If a child shows interest in a sport, especially one that stresses personal achievements rather than overly aggressive competition, a parent should seek out instructive classes or clubs, offer transportation and encourage their child's friends to participate. The focus of exercise should be fun and well-being, not winning, and the end result is a fit body, which contributes to proper physical development and self-esteem.

Sports also allows for socialization in a healthy atmosphere. Friendships with teammates and coaches are created. Set hours of interaction — practice and playing — are established and finding common ground is easy to do. Other forms of healthy socialization, such as teen clubs, an after-school job and volunteer work should be emphasized by the parents. All these activities stress positive relationships and goals. The teenagers will be surrounded by worthwhile ventures that will teach them responsibility, "esprit de corps" and the benefits of hard work.

This will also teach them the joy of giving. Working to help others, not just yourself, is an exercise that first begins in the mind and then is transformed into action. Knowing that giving of your time, energy and spirit will only strengthen the love of self is something that must be instilled by the parents. Parents should teach their children to be contributors to life; to help a spirit in trouble will lend them a wealth of pride and understanding. To replace on the earth some of what they have taken will insure a legacy for future generations. And to give love and charity to others who need it only means that that love will find its way back to the giver tenfold.

A lesson of humanity is that the takers always finish their lives with nothing, while the giver ends life with everything. In other words, a person shall reap what they sow.

Exercise in and of itself is as important as the food we take in. The physical maintenance of the body allows for a spirit filled with energy and rid of toxins. It frees the mind and lets all the functions take place properly. Children have to be taught the importance of running and playing early, then encouraged to express themselves through movement later in life.

A wealth of activities that include exercise are available today. Soccer, gymnastics, ballet, track and field, swimming, running, baseball, martial arts and yoga are just a few of the practices a youth can enjoy. Introduce children to the variety and let them choose what interests them. Then let them go!

Not to be forgotten: Exercise and positive socialization should be topped off and even enhanced by a proper diet. Although the teen years are definitely a time for maturing, the body of a teen is still not completely developed, so nutrition remains a high priority.

As in infanthood, children and teenagers should be offered the same wholesome, organic, biodynamic foods.

When possible, adults should ask their children what kinds of fruits, vegetables and healthy snacks they would prefer, so the teens can have input and make choices regarding a healthy diet. Even in regards to food, remember to respect their choices and work with their decisions.

Chapter Seventeen

●●●●●●

Family, Generations and Love

Parenthood. Can we mold and build another human being? For most of the world, that question is not a challenge, but a destiny. Somewhere in a man's life, his greatest need is to allow himself the freedom of knowing how blessed he is to be alive.

How can we not pass that blessing on?

For some, obtaining unnecessary possessions and positions of modern times cloud the meaning of life. It is important for people to understand the process of humanity and the role that conception, childhood and parenthood play in it. It is even more important to experience the spirituality of creating, having and rearing a soul that will hold in their greatest esteem your word and knowledge.

First, the choice to have children is not ours. We take it for granted that children will always be born to us. That is not always true. Ultimately, the decision rests with the children. If they are ready to come to earth, they will do so. If not, they won't. Think of children as floating souls ready to descend upon this planet when they feel they are needed or sometimes when they are wanted.

The role as parents is to allow the child a proper environment in which to develop as a human being. What less can we do for our child and the human race than to make sure that the child is sustained on the best possible foods, allowed to explore in the best possible wonderlands and exposed to the best possible education and lessons of life, mission, quality and love?

Parenthood is the most important role a person will ever play in their lives. The responsibility of that role is not only to the child, but also to the future to which that child will contribute. A child that is lacking will create a lacking world and contribute to a lacking universe.

Children who are satisfied, full and loving will give their gifts to the world and love the earth and the high power for the life they have received. Happiness will be their mainstay.

For that reason, the closest bond a person will form will be to their children. Unlike the spouse, children are of themselves, their genes, their creation, their gift of purity and kindness left to the world.

Parent-child relationships are some of the complicated ones to date. Pressure, resentment, anger, jealousy and ignorance lead to a mass meltdown of understanding.

Resolving these differences and establishing clear dialogues between generations is one of the most important things any family member can do. Love and respect are the keys to a more giving, healthy family relationship and should be exercised to the betterment of the spirit and the soul.

Without the basis that is the family, and without the support that is the first and most crucial that we experience, all is lost. We must concentrate on our goals of living life as it should be lived, with a conscious mind taking in all that is good and right and repelling all that is bad and detrimental.

It is within our power to control our destinies and shape our worlds. If we decide to take this challenge in the proper direction, we will reap the extraordinary benefits of health, clarity, respect, security and most important of all — love!

Chapter Eighteen

●●●●●●

Illness and Disease:
The Natural Medicines

We live in a sea of germs. As a result, we are constantly waging war against these microscopic disease organisms, called microorganisms or microbes. For the most part, our bodies successfully defend us. Only a very small number of microbes — called pathogens — consistently cause disease. Most microorganisms become infectious only when the body's defenses break down. (30) When these invading germs manage to penetrate the protective mucus membranes of the body and travel into internal tissues, they multiply and cause infections.

Germs and parasites are the largest concern in children's health. It is estimated in North America that 80 percent of our children are infected with parasites. Parasite infection is from a multitude of causes, the most notable being fish, then meat, then dairy products. Yet one can contract them from unwashed fruits and vegetables. And this only the beginning.

The use of unwashed utensils, tables and furniture, and of course, human contact are also potential dangers. The pinworm can even be contracted through breathing in airborne eggs. Other paths into the body include insect bites, transmission from pregnant woman to fetus via placenta and through broken skin. (31)

Some diseases that are common in animals can also infect people. Farm animals are sources of a number of infections that can be transmitted to humans, either directly or through consumption of contaminated milk or meat. For example, tapeworms, brucellosis, salmonellosis, trichinosis and toxoplasmosis can be spread through undercooked, nonpasteurized or contaminated food products.(32)

The incubation period of an infectious disease is the time between a person's exposure to the disease organism and the development of the first symptoms. Most infectious diseases have a consistent, defined incubation period. For example, almost every child will break out in the characteristic rash of chicken pox within 2 or 3 weeks after he or she has been exposed to the virus. (33)

Diarrhea, constipation, cramps and nausea are only the obvious signs of parasites. A weakened immune system gives all opportunistic diseases easy access. Every form of disease could have parasites at its origin or at least as a great contributor to its existence. Very rarely do the conventional methods of medical diagnosis detect these culprits. It takes health care professionals with keen interest, experience and sophisticated laboratories who are also trained in diagnostic technology.

Parasites and infections are generally treated through a clean lifestyle and strong anti-parasitic herbal medication, which should be used in a 10-day cycle — taking five days off and repeating the 10-day cycle. At times, with a strong infection, allopathic and herbal medication must be used together. All of these treatments must be followed by a routine of healthy bacteria flora. A healthy immune system can cope well with most infections. A compromised immune system, as a result of diseases such as cancer or AIDS, may allow usually harmless organisms to proliferate and cause widespread, serious disease.

To prevent many infections, follow this set of simple rules: When possible, stay away from anyone with a respiratory infection. Teach your children to cover their mouths and noses with a tissue when they sneeze or cough; avoid hand contact with anyone with a respiratory infection; wash your hands regularly with soap and water, particularly before meals and after using the toilet. Keep your hands away from your mouth; do not pick at your blemishes; you may spread an infection to other places; thoroughly clean and cover cuts and wounds; all serious cuts and all animal or human bites require medical attention; and avoid eating in places that have noticeably poor standards of hygiene. (34)

Listed next are natural medications for ailments that are common throughout childhood. Instead of drugstores and prescriptions, most of these remedies can be found from the earth and can be administered with help from the staff at the Institute.

For fever, sore throats and coughs, rest is very important. Golden seal and echinechea are natural antibiotics. Also una de gato used in low dosage for a few days will boost the immune system. Mix 1 tablespoon of slippery elm with a small amount of cayenne pepper to 1 pint of lemon water and drink . Before bedtime make a full, very warm bath of 1/2 cup of ground ginger, add 10 drops eucalyptus and let your child sit 15 minutes and then shower off the ginger solution.

For earaches, dip a cotton ball into 1/3 of pressed garlic mixed with 2/3 oil and position gently into outer ear. When using ice, always place the ice in a wet cloth. It will decrease swelling and pain.

For sore gums, rub a few drops of tea tree oil on the gums.

For skin irritations, use fresh or bottled aloe gel.

For stomachaches, which can be due to too many mixtures in the diet, rub castor oil on the stomach and cover with a towel. Use hot water bottle for a half hour and give enzymes and peppermint tea.

For colic, one teaspoon of psyllium or flax seeds soaked in four times their amount of water for a few hours before using should be given a few times a day. For a complete acidophilus, use 1/2 teaspoon twice a day.

For chicken pox, measles and heat rash, before bedtime, combine 1 cup of sea salt with 1 pound of aluminum-free baking soda in a warm bath and let the child sit in this for 15 minutes. Shower off afterward. It is very important to nourish the child with green juices made from sprouts, and green vegetables, as they are very rich in beta-carotene and have been successfully used to treat measles and chicken pox.

For diarrhea, use green juices, algae and some psyllium seed to soak up the fluid in the stool. Clay can also be used in small amounts to stop diarrhea. Diarrhea can lead to electrolyte imbalance, a direct link to the mineral intake in cells.

For constipation, take 1/4 psyllium or flax seeds soaked in 3/4 water and let the mixture sit for a few hours. Take as needed. Also a fiber-rich diet will prevent this illness.

Chapter Nineteen

●●●●●●

The End:
A Summary of healthy Childhood Living

Here is a summarized list of your quick reference of the healthy elements of your child's life from fetus to teenager:

The Fetus

Food — For the mother, a well-balanced diet with lots of organically grown fresh greens, sprouts, grains, nuts and seeds and fruits, and two green juices a day made of green vegetables and sprouts. Take only food-grown supplements like algae and B12, kelp and enzymes for digestion. Fried foods, alcohol, smoking, coffee and drugs should absolutely be avoided. To relieve nausea or morning sickness, try raspberry or ginger tea.

Sleep —For the mother, a nice long sleep with open windows for fresh air for about 7 to 9 hours, which is necessary for a good, healthy baby.

Exercise — With all the changes that happen to a woman when she is pregnant, it is very important that she exercises daily, walking, swimming, etc., all in moderation wearing loose, natural fiber clothes.

Enrichment — Daily singing and talking to the fetus is productive. The mother needs a lot of positive help around her. Happy moments make the pregnancy the best time of her life.

Media entertainment — The mother should only view nonviolent, heart-filled movies and television productions, such as nature films, positive autobiographies, upbeat love stories and inspirational progress.

Time of birth — Home births, water births with experienced midwife and hospital natural birthing centers have proven to be the most appropriate and positive environment for the child to enter. During delivery, play soft inspirational music and have only those people who support and love you in the room at the time of birth. At the delivery of the child, mother can use St. Johnswort oil and lubricate vaginal walls to ease the delivery and then use the oil all over the baby after the first bath.

Infant

Food — Mother's milk is the infant's natural food and bonds the baby to the mother. It is the easiest to digest, perfect nourishment, that also protects from infection, and should be consumed for a minimum of two years. It should be the child's main source of food — if not their only source of food — if healthy breast milk is available. Avoid use of drugs, smoking and alcohol, as it will enter the mother's milk. To increase milk, make sure to drink a lot of fluids and consume sprouted grains, mineral-rich root vegetables and dark green vegetables, sea and fresh water algae. The only addition after one year should be organic ripe fruit and whole organic sprout and fruit juice.

This is a great recipe for a tea to increase the mother's milk: take same amount of fennel seed and dill fruits and vervain wort, crush in the mortar or in a mill, use 1 teaspoon of the herb to 1 cup of water, boil and let sit covered for five to 10 minutes, and drink two to three times a day. You can also try the old Italian wives' tale advice to make onion soup!

Sleep — Infants should be able to sleep whenever they desire and as long as they desire within reason.

Exercise — There is no substitute for the security found in a parent with adequate self-esteem, who acts as a great mentor toward their new human friend. We would suggest reading books by Glen

Dolman, of the Center for Human Potential, on childhood development and the importance of movement and exercise. For the infant's comfort, use natural cotton diapers and natural fiber clothes.

Enrichment — Classical music and reading classics, such as Thoreau and Whitman, will begin to develop a broad consciousness at an early age which they will definitely understand. Playing music to your infant, singing and dancing, looking into their eyes will heighten their sense of self-values and happiness.

Media and entertainment — The infant should only view positive films and TV productions that include color action and happiness, excluding violence, denigration or conflict.

Toddler

Food — It is important that the toddler begins their day with algae supplement, washed down with fresh organic fruit juice (diluted 1/3 fruit juice to 2/3 distilled water). Snacks should be of organic fruit or vegetables that should be whole minus the pits or seeds. Lunch and dinner should consist of raw green salad, including sprouts, sprouted and raw grains and beans, which at times the parent may choose to cook, sweet potatoes, root vegetables, or squash, either eaten raw or blended, or at times baked or steamed.

The maximum of the cooked food should be 25 percent by weight.

Sleep — There is no doubt that the toddler requires between 10 and 12 hours of sleep a day including daily naps.

Exercises — Toddlers should be encouraged to join into family exercise, including daily use of a trampoline. The toddler should have an endless availability for physical activity.

Enrichment — Adult contemporary classical music and native people music as well as folk and positive children compositions will lift the child to new levels of awareness.

Media entertainment — It is not too early to expose a toddler to fine film and television productions, theater and appropriate concerts that are colorful, humorous and positive, devoid of violent conflict and friction.

Child

Food — The child should be eating the same healthy food that the parents should be eating — organically grown whole sprouted grains, beans, legumes, seeds and nuts, vegetables, including root vegetables, winter squash and all forms of fruit that have been vine and tree-ripened and juices made from fruits (mix 1/3 juice to 2/3 water) and juices from sprouts and green vegetables. Distilled or reverse osmosis water. Dehydrated vegetables and nuts (roasted nut substitute) air-popped popcorn, baked not fried chips, and whole grain crackers round out a fine menu for a healthy and active child. The child could be eating equal amounts of food as the parent, and this is not considered abnormal due to their growth and energy needs.

Sleep — In most cases, the child requires more than eight hours of sleep and it would not be considered abnormal if the child sleeps 10 hours or more. This is also due to metabolism, growth and energy consumption.

Exercise —The child should be encouraged to have boundless freedom to explore all forms of exercise including competitive sports, dance, gymnastics, etc. Family activity, such as roller blading, volleyball, tennis and water activities will help their developing bodies and mind.

Enrichment — Your child will begin to develop their own sense of culture and at times may bring music and film into the family setting that may not be appealing to you. Providing that it is not negative and denigrating, you should bite your tongue and encourage the developing identity. At home, exposing your child to classical music and theater, fine literature and positive films and television production will create an anchor in their future.

Media entertainment — Peer pressure will begin where the child may be encouraged by friends to view violent and destructive visual "entertainment." A parent must be strong but gentle in explaining the reasons the child should not view such mutation of the human spirit. Always offer positive options.

Teenager

Food — A teenager should eat all the foods that the parent should be eating — all organically grown vegetables, fruits, sprouted grains, beans, legumes, soaked seeds and nuts , root vegetables, yams, winter squash, breads made of sprouted whole grains, and juices made from the sprouts and vegetables or fruits. This should be their main staple which is provided at home and encouraged when socializing. Make sure they have economic means and the locations of healthy food restaurants. Constant dialogue throughout the child's life will enable the teenager to have a strong foundation and understanding that they should be consuming healthy foods. Your example is the best teacher.

Sleep — Most teenagers require the same sleep that the parent does, yet teenagers tend to be very active and avoid healthy sleeping patterns. Encourage them to sleep so their still developing bodies can acquire a strong immune system.

Exercise — At this point, most teenagers have particular tastes when it comes to physical activity. You should encourage all exercise activity and hopefully, still be able to influence your young adults, participation in family activities.

Enrichment — It is common that a teenager will be bringing loud and jarring music and visual entertainment into the home. You as a parent should not create conflict over this unless it is degrading, violent, or vividly sexual. If you as a parent have provided conscious musical and visual art to your child throughout his or her life, he or she will still be influenced in a positive way and will return to a more stable stage of consciousness after their natural developmental resistant stage.

Media — It is quite normal for a teenager to be attracted to sexual and action-packed visual entertainment. As a parent, your role should be a totally candid guide about sex and violence, and the positive and negative aspects of these critical subjects.

Family development and thoughts on practical aspects of life:

* Family traveling can create a bonding experience that is unsurpassed. Experiencing new places, people and events together will give common ground for a full lifetime relationship.

*   Always being a friend with ability to give non-confronting advice to your child will enable you to help to create a successful and happy future for your child and a lifelong friend for yourself.

*   Speaking about God, the Universe and people's roles with them will allow a young person the freedom to feel that they are part of a phenomenal, symbiotic life which makes them understand that they are not alone and they have the support of the higher realm. We all need to feel that we can rely on the energy of the spirit to accomplish many of our difficult goals.

*   Intelligence is not created through education. It is created through the development of the intellect. We must nurture learning through instinct rather than teaching by demand. This will give your child the ability to make clear and competent decisions throughout his or her life.

*   Within each moment that we spend openly with our young friends, we share further moments of happiness with them.

*   Allowing opportunities for your child to be challenged rather than overprotecting them

will permit personal development and self-esteem.

* When a child displays their particular artistic interests, be it painting, dance or music, encourage them by making available lessons and experiential opportunity.

* Hugging, kissing and massage should be a part of your family's experience which allows the child to feel loved, healthy and secure.

* When possible, spend as much time with positive relatives and positive friends to give them a sense of family and community and establishing their sense of belonging which many of us are missing in our mobile society.

* When choosing an educational setting, try to find a school which emphasizes individual development, the raising of self-esteem, and social and cultural awareness. In certain situations, home schooling with the addition of home school group activities and family outings can be appropriate. Those who are fortunate to reside in a community with progressive schools should utilize and support these institutions.

References

1. Bode, Janet. *Kids Having Kids; The Unwed Teenage Parent.* 1980. Franklin Watts Publication, New York. Book jacket.
2. *Kids Having Kids*, p. 16.
3. *Kids Having Kids*, p. 23.
4. Arthur, Shirley. *Surviving Teen Pregnancy; Your Choices, Dreams and Decisions.* 1991. Morning Glory Press, Buena Park, CA. p. 61
5. *Surviving Teen Pregnancy*, p. 54-57.
6. Eisenburg, Arlene; Murkoff, Heidi E.; Hathaway, Sandee E. *What to Expect When You're Expecting.* 1991. Workman Publishing Co. Inc., New York. p. 28-29. (a) Klaper, Michael, M.D. Pregnancy, Children and the Vegan Diet. 1987. Gentle World Inc., Paia, Maui. p. 4(b) Vegan. p. 4-5
7. Wilson, Josleen. *The Pre-Pregnancy Planner.* 1986. Doubleday & Co. Inc., Garden City, New York. p.4.
8. *The Pre-Pregnancy Planner*, p. 5.
9. *What to Expect.* p. 382.
10. Kitzinger, Sheila. *The Complete Book of Pregnancy and Childbirth.* 1988. Alfred A. Knopf, New York. p. 84
11. *The Complete Book*, p. 84.
12. *What to Expect*, p. 251-253.
13. *What to Expect*, p. 254.
14. *What to Expect*, p. 254.
15. Atwood, Stephen J., M.D. *A Doctor's Guide to Feeding Your Child; Complete Nutrition for Healthy Growth.* 1982. MacMillan Publishing Co., Inc. New York. p. 29.

16. *What to Expect*, p. 255

17. *A Doctor's Guide*, p. 69

18. *A Doctor's Guide*, p. 72.

19. *A Doctor's Guide*, p. 69-70.

20. *A Doctor's Guide*, p. 72.

21. Eisenburg, Arlene; Murkoff, Heidi E.; Hathaway, Sandee E. *What to Expect The First Year.* 1989. Workman Publishing Co. Inc., New York. p. 206.

22. *What to Expect—First Year*, p. 206-207.

23. *The Pre-Pregnancy Planner*, p. 26.

24. *The Pre-Pregnancy Planner*, p. 26.

25. *The Pre-Pregnancy Planner*, p. 26.

26. Ginot, Hain G. *Between Parent and Child.* 1956. Avon Books, New York. p. 51.

27. *11 Million Teenagers: What Can Be Done About the Epidemic of Adolescent Pregnancies in the United States*, a publication of The Alan Guttmacher Institute, New York. p. 9

28. V. Masters and N. Lehman. *Masters and Johnson Explained.* 1976. Chicago: Playboy Press. p. 163-164.

29. Melton, David. *Survival Kit for Parents of Teenagers.* 1979. St. Martin's Press, New York. p. 27.

30. The American Medical Association. *The Battle Against Infection.* The Reader's Digest Association Inc., Pleasantville, New York/Montreal, 1992. p. 9

31. AMA. p. 10.

32. AMA. p. 11

33. AMA. p.14.

34. AMA. p. 16-17.

Reference for
Positive Children's Books:

Exchange Publishing
120 Hawthorne
Palo Alto, California 94301

Suggested Music:

Return to Pooh Corner
by Kenny Loggins
on Sony Records

Hippocrates Health Insitute Offers an Unsurpassed Health Vacation

You are invited to attend our in-house guest program, which will teach you how to make exercise and healthful eating a part of your daily routine. For four decades people have been acquiring the needed education and motivation to change their inappropriate exercise and eating habits by spending this valuable time with us. Several weeks is the usual length of our program, but longer or shorter stays can be arranged. For more information you may call or write to our reservations clerk.

For those of you who desire involvement in the health field our Health Educator Course is considered by many in the field to be one of the most complete, state-of-the-art progressive health educations available anywhere. The pace is fast and the instructors are demanding, but the rewards more than compensate. Contact us for complete details regarding this eight-week health experience.

For four decades Hippocrates Health Institute has offered literature, tapes (audio and video), juicers and health equipment, along with whole food supplements, all of which are available to you with a call to the Institute.

Hippocrates Health Institute
1443 Palmdale Court
West Palm Beach, Florida 33411
(407) 471-8876